A Practical Guide Into the Insights of Prophesying

The Office of the Prophet, Prophetic Ministry & Judging Prophecy

---

Prophet Jermaine Johnson

A PRACTICAL GUIDE INTO THE INSIGHTS OF PROPHESYING: The Office of the Prophet, Prophetic Ministry & Judging Prophecy
Copyright © 2015 by Jermaine Johnson

Published by Vision Directives

All rights reserved. No part of this book may be reproduced or transmitted in any form or by any means without written permission from the author.

ISBN: 978-0692394762

Printed in USA

Dedication

I dedicate this manual first and foremost to my LORD and SAVIOR JESUS CHRIST who saved, delivered, and called me into the prophetic ministry. I also want to thank my spiritual parents in the gospel, Apostle Ivory Hopkins and his wife Minister Evelyn Hopkins; also Apostle Levin Bailey and his wife Minister Rose Bailey for raising me up in the gospel and teaching me the things of the kingdom of God.

I want to say to my parents Johnnie Johnson and Cynthia Neal for always being there for me, love you guys! To my children Vincent, Jeshale, and Charity - love you guys. Finally last but not least to my wife of 19 years Roberta Johnson and counting - thanks for always supporting me and the vision God put within me. I love you sweetheart!!!

Table of Contents

Foreword 5

Introduction 7

Section I: Prophesying 9

Personal Testimony 12

Section II: The Gift of the Prophet 19

Section III: Prophetic Ministries and Prophetic Teams 39

Section IV: Judging Prophecy 50

Conclusion 61

Foreword

God has truly blessed me to have a part in mentoring an awesome man of God, Jermaine Johnson. Jermaine came into my life about 19 years ago. A young man hungry for God, a young man that did not have a first class pass but the opposite; He was a young man that had been in prison but now was a man that loved God.

Jermaine came to Pilgrims' Ministry of Deliverance at the beginning of his recovery of a rough pass. His love for God has caused him to grow in God at a swift rate. Jermaine flows strong in the prophetic and he is an excellent teacher of the Word of God. He now pastors Prophetic Kingdom Ministry which he and his wife founded. I am so proud of Pastor Jermaine Johnson and his lovely wife Prophetess Roberta Johnson.

A Practical Guide Into the Insight of Prophesying: The Office of the Prophet, Prophetic Ministries, and Judging Prophecy, will be a blessing to all that will draw from the anointing that is upon this manual. You will come away with knowledge of the prophetic, how to operate in the prophetic, how to hear and recognize the voice of God and much more.

May God bless you in whatever ministry assignment you have and you being faithful to God and his church until He returns

With much Love and Respect, and Appreciation

Apostle Levin V. Bailey

Pilgrim's Ministry Of Deliverance

Foreword (con't)

Prophet Jermaine Johnson is one of my Son's in the Gospel who has a profound insight of the prophetic calling and ministry. In this book, you will gain practical biblical knowledge on how to operate in the prophetic ministry and walk in prophetic protocol that will make your gifting acceptable in church ministry.

It has been a pleasure to have been a part of the development of such balanced prophetic teacher as Pastor/Prophet Jermaine Johnson.

Apostle Ivory L. Hopkins (aka The General of Deliverance)
Overseer and founder of Pilgrims Ministry of Deliverance
East Coast Chancellor of Rapha Deliverance University

Introduction

This manual is a guide for a practical understanding of prophesying, the prophet's office, prophetic ministries and judging prophecy. I believe this manual will impart wisdom and give a better understanding of these awesome gifts God has placed in the body of Christ through the will of his Holy Spirit. I hope it will inspire you to seek and search for and after all that our heavenly Father, Jesus Christ, and the Holy Spirit has for us, the church.

I was inspired to write this manual to help others to reach their full potential through simplistic practical teachings that are in the word of God and through my own personal life testimonies as a maturing prophet of God who governs a prophetic ministry. My prayer is that the eyes of your understanding be opened and your spirits illuminated with revelation, wisdom, knowledge and understanding. I also pray that God will continue to raise up true prophets, prophetic people and prophetic ministries with the spirit of excellence who will carry the torch of his glory throughout this earth and that our Father's kingdom will be established on earth as it is in heaven.

I have one agenda, to finish the work God has given me to finish and to leave this earth when it is time - empty. I want to be able to make the statement like Apostle Paul did in 2 Timothy when he said, "I have fought a good fight I have kept the faith and I have finished my course". This manual is a part of my prophetic destiny to empower others when it comes to the prophetic, the prophetic ministry and its operations and to teach the wisdom of God concerning the prophetic and the order God has put in place for His church. There will be false operations just like with any gift but the true will prevail and this manual will help enlighten you to be able to recognize the difference.

So get ready to discover the prophetic like never before and be ready to be stretched in the spirit beyond what you have before, through the simplicity of the gospel that will lead you to deeper spiritual places in the spirit. Let us enjoy this journey together as God leads us by the Holy Spirit.

-Prophet Jermaine Johnson

SECTION I: PROPHESYING

1. Prophesying is the speaking forth by divine inspirations, to predict, to utter forth, to declare a thing which can only be known by divine revelation, with the idea of foretelling future events pertaining especially to the kingdom of God.

2. To sum it all up prophesying is being inspired by God to speak about past, present, or future happenings.

3. 1 Cor. 14:3 says, "Follow after charity and desire spiritual gifts but rather that ye may prophesy". 1 Thess. 5:20 says, "Despise not prophesying".

4. We are to desire the gifts of the spirit and especially the God given ability to prophesy. Why? Because Apostle Paul lets us know in 1 Cor.14:4 in the latter half of the verse "but he that prophesieth edifies the church so therefore this gift should not be despised" (to make no account of or to utterly despise).

5. When someone is prophesying they will speak words of edification (building), exhortation (a calling near) or comfort (to console). However, prophets go beyond the basics of general prophesying which we will discuss in detail in the next section of this prophetic manual.

6. Prophesying can also be accompanied with the gifts of word of wisdom and word of knowledge (1 Cor. 12:8). The difference in these two gifts are simple: the word of knowledge deals with past and present events while the word of wisdom deals with future events or something that was not previously known. Also at times the discerning of spirits mentioned in 1 Cor. 12:10, which speaks for itself, "the discerning or distinguishing or judging what spirit is in operation whether it be God, the devil or the human spirit"; which we will discuss later in the manual.

7. We are also told to covet to prophesy in 1Cor.14:39. Notice we are not told to covet the prophet even though that should be received if they are true prophets of God because there is a reward in doing that (Matt. 10:42). We are also not told to covet prophecy, even though if it is from God it should be received. We are told to covet to prophesy or can we say, to burn with zeal be eager, desire earnestly, pursue, strive after to be a prophetic

voice used by God for his kingdom. Many people want to hear a personal word for themselves and that is good but God wants to use us for his glory!

They tell me that a president (I believe it was JFK) once said, "Ask not what your country can do for you but what can you do for your country." God is looking for vessels that will rise up from that low place of receiving into a higher blessed place of giving. We can get stagnant in the kingdom of God when we focus on the well of our salvation (John 4:14) only and forget about the rivers of living waters (John 7:38). I want to be a river and say what Isaiah said, "Here I am Lord send me!"

8. God is raising up people who will be a prophetic voice in the earth, who will promote his kingdom his rule, reign, authority, power and glory. People who like Moses, that will not be satisfied until they see the glory of God manifested. God is calling us higher. He is releasing his glory in the earth like never before. He is restoring the apostolic and the prophetic gift back to His body for His glory. As He said in Jeremiah He is saying today, "before I formed you in the belly of your mother I knew you and before you came out of the womb I sanctified you I set you apart and I ordained you or purposed you to be a prophet to the nations" (Jer. 1:5). He also inspired Apostle Paul to write in Ephesians 1:4, "That according as he hath chosen us in him before the foundation of the world, that we should be holy and without blame before him in love." In other words, you were destined to be what God has called you to be before you were conceived by your parents and even before day you were born months later. We are that chosen generation, royal priesthood, holy nation, peculiar people (his purchased possession) which He purchased with blood to shew forth the praises of him who called us out of darkness into his marvelous light (1 Peter 2:9). So let us be a mouth piece for God and prophesy as we are inspired (stirred up on the inside; prompted) to do so.

9. I want to make two things clear. One I don't believe we can prophesy anytime we want to that is false teaching. The bible says in 2 Peter 1:21, "For prophecy came not in old time by the will of man: but holy men of God spake as they were moved (to be moved inwardly or prompted) by the Holy Ghost." So it is not by our own doing we yield to

what the Spirit of God wants to do through us. People, who operate outside of God's Spirit, are moving towards and are practicing witchcraft. I always say, "You have to have an unction to function or there will be a malfunction." I also believe based on the bible and what we discuss further in this manual under the section judging prophecy, that people can miss God. Now that does not make them a false prophet or false prophetic messenger that makes them a human who is not perfect and can make mistakes even though they are gifted by a perfect God. We learn from those mistakes and we mature and develop. All prophecy must be judged for this reason.

10. The second thing I want to make clear is that just because we may prophesy it does not mean we are called to be prophets, which is a fivefold ministry gift (we will discuss this further in the next section of this manual). Being a prophet is not something we choose for ourselves it is something Jesus gave to some in his church (Ephesians 4:11). I emphasize the word "**some**" not all, but some. We must get that in our minds. You must also never chase after something God did not call you to do. Apostle Paul said in 1 Cor. 10:13, "Know your measure of rule distributed to you by God concerning your purpose and calling." In other words like a driver driving a car down a single lane road, stay in your lane and know your boundaries. Being ourselves and doing God's will for our lives will help us to reach our full potential so when we die or when Jesus returns for us we will have emptied out everything he put in us to do.

PERSONAL TESTIMONY

In my personal testimony I did not start prophesying in the church I started at home. During my times at home of praying in tongues and not understanding what was going on I began wondering if I was losing my mind. Interestingly enough, I was losing my mind and I was gaining the mind of Christ. Daily I would speak in tongues, and one day after being baptized in the Holy Ghost, my tongues were followed by English words! These were not words I thought but words I was divinely inspired to say by an inward tugging and burning. Now this may be happening to some of you, and if so, don't be afraid. God is revealing Himself to you. Yield to Him. He won't force you but He will compel you to yield; so yield and allow Him to speak through you. Like in 2 Timothy 1:6 you are stirring up the gift of God that is in you. The word *stir* means; to kindle up so you can bring what God wants out of you; that treasure that is in earthen vessels for his glory!

I also was and still am today a committed member of a local body of believers with strong bible doctrine being taught. My spiritual leaders didn't suppress the gifts in me but encouraged their development and growth through biblical training as well as demonstration. They, along with myself hearing from God, recognized the call of God on my life to prophesy, be a prophet, and operate a prophetic ministry. God did not call us to be separate from the rest of the body. We are many members but one body. No one is on an island to themselves. We need God ordained leadership who will help release God's people into their prophetic destiny.

I Thank God for the dedicated leaders I have had in my life and I'm grateful to God for them. Now let us go on to explore the gift of the prophet given by the Prophet above all prophets - Jesus himself.

Notes:_____
_____
_____
_____

SECTION II: THE GIFT OF THE PROPHET

1. A Prophet is an interpreter of the oracles or of hidden things. One who moves by the Spirit of God and hence His organ or spokesman. A prophet solemnly declares to men what he has received by inspiration especially concerning future events and in particular such as relates to the cause and the kingdom of God and to human salvation.

2. In Ephesians 4:11 Apostle Paul writes, "and he gave some apostles, and some prophets and some evangelists and some pastors and teachers." Notice here the word "some" again; not all but some. Not everybody is called to the divine office (function) of being a prophet. It is a gift from Jesus who was *that Prophet* that God told Moses about in Deut. 18 that was like unto himself. This gift can't be bought or earned; it is given. The bible states in 1 Cor. 12:29, "Are all apostles? Are all prophets? Are all teachers?" The answer is emphatically, NO!

3. We must fully understand prophets are called by God and inspired by God when to speak on His behalf. Everything God says to us is not meant to be said to others or at that particular time. Let us be like the children of Issachar knowing the times and seasons for what their nation should be doing (1 Chronicles 12:32). We must remember, we are God's ambassador. He is not our ambassador. We speak for Him. He is not our spokesman. In other words, let us be let by the Spirit of God when it comes to His Spiritual Gifts.

PURPOSES OF THE PROPHET

1. The prophet is a gift with a divine purpose. The prophet is much more than a person who just prophesies (which they do) however, they have a particular function that they are equipped to fulfill in the body of Christ, for the development of the church.

2. We will find this purpose and function in Ephesians 4:12 which states, "for the perfecting of the saints, for the work of the ministry, to the edifying of the body of Christ."

3. A prophet has a responsibility to perfect the saints. The word *perfect* here means to: completely furnish, equip or a bringing to maturity; especially concerning the ministry of a prophet and the developing of prophetic gifts. Many people are gifted to prophesy but many are unlearned and unskilled when it comes to understanding their gifts and callings. It would be like driving a car with no sense of direction of where you are going and how to get there. God said in the book of Hosea 4:6, *"my people perish from the lack of knowledge"* and He also said *"they reject my knowledge."* No one person knows it all. We all can be taught and as we apply what we are taught we will grow in His knowledge and grace. Prophets just don't prophesy they are also preachers and teachers perfecting the saints.

4. Why are the saints being perfected? The answer is for the work of the ministry. The work of the ministry is the service of God's work inside and outside our worship, assembly places. Yes God has called his church to work, to labor, not just to come to a building to enjoy ourselves but to actually learn how to be effective for his kingdom. So the prophet has a purpose to mature the saints and empower them to do the works of God within and without to establish the kingdom.

5. Not only are the saints perfected to do the work; the end result is to edify the body of Christ. In other words, the church will be built up they, will be strengthened and expanded, so we can become that unified, blood washed, faith filled, powerful

demonstrating church that won't be drawn away by false teaching and doctrine. Instead, by the truth of the gospel of Jesus of Christ spoken in love, will grow every way God desires finding our spiritual place of authority in the body - our proper place and the body building itself up in love (Ephesians 4:11-16). Prophets have the responsibility to preach and teach the body of Christ biblical truth for their spiritual growth. We must not preach our own opinions or the traditions of men but the word of the living God.

6. A prophet is God's divine mouthpiece to speak what He wants released in the earth concerning people, places, and things. Whether it is concerning world leaders, widows, children, territories, nations and at times even concerning nature and its creatures. Amos 3:7 says, "Surely the Lord God will do nothing, but first he revealeth his secrets unto his servants the prophets." I know there are some secrets things that belong to God but the things that he does reveal are for us and our children (Deut. 29:29). For example, no one except the Father knows when Jesus is returning (Matt. 24:36). Men have tried to predict this to their own destruction and the destruction of their followers. God has not and will not reveal this to any man. There will be signs of the end being near and I believe we are closer than ever before, but no man knows - period. However the secrets that God does reveal to us he uses his prophets to do it.

7. I want to reiterate that prophets are also preachers or teachers or both. Let me state this boldly, *"any prophet who can't rightly divide the word of truth is a danger to themselves and the ones who will listen to them."* If we don't know what the bible says then how can we effectively do what the bible tells us to do? The word is our map and without its direction we will be led into deception and damage people in the process (Psalms 119:105). I'm very passionate about this particular subject because it is not about having a title pronounced in front of our names; it is about lifting up the name of Jesus and ministering to his people and we must take it very serious. We can't teach others if we are not learning ourselves.

8. Prophets can also be called to nations, regions, or to a local group of people. It depends on God's purpose and call for their lives. Everyone does not have the same

calling. We must stay in our assigned calling knowing that it is not about fame or fortune but being carriers of God's glory.

9. Prophets can also be pastors of their own local ministries. Jeremiah 17:16 says, "as for me I have not hastened from being a pastor to follow thee:" so prophets can operate in more than one fivefold ministry gift as we see here with Jeremiah. Jeremiah was a prophet and he functioned as a pastor to God's people. Once again everyone's calling is different and this is not the standard of rule for every prophet. I happen to be a prophet/pastor myself with an apostolic call on my life. There are also others like this in the body of Christ. Don't let other people limit what God has put in you.

10. Prophets can also release words of prosperity over people's lives as they are led by the Holy Spirit. I'm not talking about money games, tricks of deceitful men or schemes conjured up in the back office of some greedy preachers, (of which I have seen a few). I'm talking about a genuine move of God's presence that releases divine provision and unlocks God's promises. 2 Chronicles 20:20 says, "Believe in the Lord God and you will be established (firm or sure) and believe his prophets and so shall ye prosper (advance, succeed, make progress, be profitable)." Also in 1 Kings 17:8-16 through the word of the prophet Elijah, God sustained a widow, her household, and Elijah by miraculously not allowing the meal in the barrel or cruise of oil to empty and they were sustained in a famine for many days. I want you to understand that Elijah didn't go to the widow by his own will, he was led by God. Notice also he didn't ask for the whole cake he said, bake me a little cake first. Her God inspired giving to Elijah, who was in need and was a prophet, released her miracle harvest. In 2 Kings 4:1-7 Elisha the successor to Elijah served Elijah by pouring water so Elijah could wash his hands. He (Elisha) received a double portion of the predecessor's anointing. A widow of the prophets came to him in debt looking for a way out because the creditors were about to take her sons. Elisha gave her prophetic instructions, that what she needed to get out of debt was already in her house. That is

also a word for someone today. God has already put what you need to be debt free in your house. In other words, on the inside of you is a God inspired idea that will give you the victory. Now getting back to Elisha and the widow, she said all she had was a pot of oil then he said, go and borrow vessels; a lot from your neighbors. She was already in debt and he told her to borrow?! Sometimes what God will tell you to do through the prophet will not make natural sense but in your obedience lay the blessings of God. She did it and every time she went to fill a vessel there was more oil in the pot until all the vessels that she had borrowed were filled. Then she went back to Elisha who said, "Now sell the oil, pay off your debt and live off the rest." True prophets can release true life changing prosperity. We have experienced this in our own ministry with people through prophetic words, getting jobs they were not qualified to get, homes they never dreamed of having and finances they had never expected. I'm not a so called prosperity preacher but I know that God uses his prophets to release and unleash his blessings.

11. The purpose of the New Testament prophet does differ from the Old Testament because we are now under grace and truth and not the law. The Old Testament prophet was who everyone would go to as God's spokesman but today God does not only speak to his prophet he speaks to his people. The Old Testament prophet came under greater condemnation - even death for speaking in God's name falsely. Under the new covenant the prophets are still accountable for what they speak in God's name but their prophetic words are judged by other prophets, mature believers and church leadership to test their authenticity. God will judge false prophets, preachers, and teachers, etc. in his own timing. However, a prophet who unintentionally or because of being prideful misspeaks God's words will be corrected. God will correct that prophet or prophet in training and encourage them to keep stepping out on faith but also give them divine wisdom. We all have made mistakes with our gifts but God is perfecting us. The problem comes when we find out we were wrong and won't receive correction from God and the authority He set up. Remember God will resist the proud but he gives more grace to the humble (1 Peter 5:5).

12. Prophets are also used to give corrective words and at times words of direction and warnings. However when it comes to direction we must remember that we are to be led by the Spirit and not the will of people; and all words must be examined. I have through divine inspiration given warnings, corrective words, and directive words and when it comes to direct words especially, I always encourage the recipients of those words to judge that word carefully because I could be just plain wrong. That is why I encourage all believers to know God's voice for themselves. Also we must understand that every prophetic word is not going to be what people want to hear, so as a prophet we have to be free from a spirit of rejection or fear of rejection. Jesus himself was not always well received (Matt. 13:53-58) and neither will true prophets of God. Many of the prophets of old were imprisoned, tortured, and not received and Jesus said in Luke 6:26, "Woe unto you when all when men speak well of you for your fathers did the same of the false prophets." We will not be liked, loved, or received by all but we must know we are loved, received, and called by God to be a prophetic voice in the earth.

13. Prophets can also help release the body of Christ into their gifts through prophetic words and the laying on of hands. 1 Timothy 4:14 says, "neglect not the gift that is in thee, which was given by prophecy, with the laying on of hands of the presbytery (team of elders)." In this case a gift was released in Timothy, Paul's son in the gospel, who was made a pastor by a team of prophetic elders. There is an order to this. We don't override church leadership but we work in unity with the church's recognized leadership that is in place.

14. Prophets also can release divine healing as well as release divine miracles by the power of God. (See 2 Kings chapters 3-6) and also (1 Kings 17:17-24).

JESUS THE PROPHET

1. Jesus himself was that prophet. He wasn't just *any* prophet or *one* of the prophets but that Prophet that John the Baptist spoke of in the gospel of Apostle John (John 1:21). Referring to Deut. 18:18 the Prophet that we should all hear, who would be like unto

Moses, because he would deliver his people; but greater than Moses because he was God in the flesh who dwelt among his people.

2. The Samaritan woman at the well in the gospel of John 4:16-19 said she perceived (knew within herself) that Jesus was a prophet because he gave her a word of knowledge concerning her past five husbands and the man she was living with who she was not married to.

3. Jesus speaking of himself in Matt. 13:57 said, "A prophet is not without honor except in his own country and household." When he went back to his hometown where he was raised but wasn't received, he could not do many healings or miracles because of their unbelief.

4. In the book of Matthew 21:10-11 it says, "And when he was to come into Jerusalem all the city was moved saying, who is this? And the multitude said this is Jesus the prophet of Nazareth of Galilee." I want to be very clear Jesus was an Apostle, Prophet, Evangelist, Pastor, and Teacher. He had the Spirit of God without measure (limit; see John 3:34) and He is God that came in the flesh and our Lord and Savior.

5. Jesus being a prophet released words of healings, miracles, and cast out devils which we find when we explore the four gospels, Matt., Mark, Luke and John. What a mighty God we serve. He also told us greater works shall we do because now He is sitting on the right hand of the Father in heaven. To him be all the glory!

DIFFERENT REALMS OF THE PROPHETIC

1. First let us define realms which according to the Webster dictionary are areas, spheres, or domains. In other words there are different areas, spheres, or domains when it comes to the prophetic ministry. Today we are going to examine and dissect the three basic realms of the prophetic.

2. The first realm of the prophetic is the spirit of prophecy. In this area of the prophetic any believer when in the midst of high worship or in the company of prophets can prophesy.

3. They are not prophets but the spirit of prophesy can come upon them and they can begin to prophesy. This has happened in the bible. 1 Samuel 10:1-12 tells about Saul being anointed the first king of Israel and how when Samuel told him he would meet a company of prophets, on his way in the city, the Spirit of the Lord would come on him, he would prophesy and be turned into another man. Saul was not a prophet but when he came into the midst of the company of prophets who were praising and worshipping God he was able to prophesy. Also in 1 Samuel 19:18-24 the servants that Saul sent to take David (whom he wanted to kill because Saul had a jealous spirit) when the servants came in the midst of the company of prophets they prophesied. He sent three different sets of servants and the Spirit of God came on them and they prophesied and Saul came to himself. He then rent his clothes and also prophesied. None of them were prophets but when the Spirit came on them they prophesied. This also happened in Numbers 11:25-29, when the Lord took the spirit that was upon Moses and put it on their seventy elders. When the Spirit of God came on them they prophesied so that Moses would not carry the burden of leadership alone. This happens many times in services where the worship is high and then someone will speak in divers tongues and they or another believer will interpret the God given message through the gift of interpretation. Both of these gifts are found in 1 Cor.12:1-10. Again, they are not all prophets even though some maybe who prophesy in services like this, but not all are prophets that the Spirit of God comes upon. In John 11:49-52 the high priest prophesied about Jesus' death not realizing what he was saying. It was God's Spirit that came on him because he was in the office of high priest. To sum it all up, Revelations 19:10 tells us to worship God for the testimony of Jesus is the Spirit of Prophecy. Once again most people who operate in the realm of the spirit of prophecy are not prophets but they do prophesy. Their prophecies are limited to edification, exhortation, and comfort (1 Cor.14:3), unless they are a true prophet who has a higher level of responsibility.
4. The second realm of the prophetic is the gift of prophecy found in 1 Cor.12:10. In this realm a person has the gift to prophecy more frequently and beyond just a high service of worship. These prophetic people prophesy a lot because they have the gift but they are

not prophets because they don't have that God ordained calling to walk in that gift office of a prophet. In this realm the person with the gift of prophecy is limited to words of edification, exhortation, and comfort just like the person who operates in the realm of the Spirit of Prophecy. The difference being the person with the gift has that gift always within them even though they still have to be God inspired to use that gift. Remember, God moves us to use us. The gift of prophecy is given to certain believer by the Holy Ghost not of their own choosing (1 Cor.12:11). In Acts 21:9 we read about Phillip the evangelist, formally one of the seven deacons in Acts 6, whose four daughters, which were virgins, prophesied or had the gift of prophesy. These daughters were not prophets but they did prophesy. In the next verse it talks about a prophet named Agabus.

5. The third realm of the prophetic is the gift or gift office of a prophet. I say gift office because it is a gift given by Jesus himself with a particular function and purpose that is ordained by God himself. We went over what a prophet is and the purposes of a prophet in the beginning of this section, now we are going to explore the differences between this office gift, the gift of prophecy and the spirit of prophecy.

Ephesians 4:11 lets us know that Jesus gave this gift to some not all in the church. So it is Jesus who determines who the "some" are, not us. According to the Webster's dictionary *an office is a special duty, charge, position of authority, position of responsibility, or service of worship.* This is how the prophet is a gift to the body of Christ and an office because they have a responsibility along with the apostle, evangelist, pastor, and teacher; to mature the saints, prepare them for work of the ministry, and help build up the body of Christ for the glory of God. Yes, prophets do prophesy. They have that gift but they have a greater responsibility to preach or teach usually both. They teach church concerning the things of the kingdom and especially the prophetic ministry and its operations and reproduce other prophetic believers. They also develop other prophets of God. In the Old Testament Samuel, Elijah, and Elisha ran what we call schools of prophets, company of prophets or sons of the prophets. They trained others in the things of God; those that had that particular calling of prophet (office) on their lives. They usually lived together but today we don't have to dwell together under the same roof however, we all need training.

Remember Acts 21:10, Agabus was called a prophet while in verse nine Phillip's four daughters had the gift to prophecy. Prophets go beyond speaking words of edification, exhortation, and comfort - to words of warning as Agabus did with Paul, to words of correction, revelation, sometimes rebuke, sometimes judgement and sometimes direction. Prophets operate not only in the inspirational gifts of prophecy, divers tongues, and interpretation but they also operate in the revelation gifts listed in 1 Cor.12:8-10; word of wisdom, word of knowledge, and discerning of spirits. Prophets also operate at times in healing and miracles as well as the gift of faith. Daniel was an example of a prophet operating in the gift of faith when he was cast into the lion's den with hungry lions and went to sleep and woke up unharmed. God used prophets such as Elijah, Elisha and unnamed prophets to perform healings and miracles. Once again prophets are preachers and teachers of the word of God with no compromising of the word. Prophets who prophesy but don't know the bible are a recipe for disaster and will help shipwreck the faith of their followers. I will continue to stress this because novices lifted up in pride will fall. A novice is a newly planted Christian who is not learned in the principles of God. Prophets have to be matured. I myself believe that true prophets of God have the God given ability to train other prophets and prophetic people and to help them walk in grace and grow in the knowledge of Jesus Christ and become laborers for God. Every prophet is different some are hearers and some are seers. In other words some hear God speak and they speak while others see in the spirit realm what God is saying. Some prophets do both. All of them have their place in the body and no one is more spiritual then the other because they are all called by God and used by God for God (1 Sam. 9:9 about a seer). There are also teams of prophets, as we talked about the company of prophets, in the Old Testament and presbytery in the New Testament. This will be discussed further in the section on Prophetic Ministries in this manual. Now we will look at the different ways God speaks to us.

THE DIFFERENT WAYS GOD SPEAKS TO US AND USES US PROPHETICALLY

1. God will use the scriptures as his primary way to speak to his people. The bible is that more sure word of prophecy according to 2 Peter 1:19-20. Hebrews 4:12 says, "…it is quick and powerful sharper than any two edged sword and will divide asunder between soul and spirit bone and marrow the intent of the heart and discerner of the thoughts." It is also a lamp unto our feet and a light unto our path (Psalms 119:105). Peter also said in his first epistle, "that we were born again not of corruptible but incorruptible by the word of God which liveth and abideth forever (1 Peter 1:24-25)." When Jesus defeated Satan in the wilderness, while he was being tempted by him, He used what was written the word (Matt.4:1-11). The word, the bible, the scriptures are the primary ways God speaks to his people. It is also the source that we go to in order to prove the other ways God speak to us and using us is truly God speaking to and through us. The Word of God is the final say concerning all the things of God even our life itself.

2. God will also use what we call a rhema or God inspired word for our situations to speak to us which we call prophecy. Prophecy itself is conditional and must always be in line with the bible are it is invalid. The Holy Spirit will never tell us to say something that violates the word of God. That is why prophecy, rather for an individual or congregation, etc., must be judged or shall I say proven. Acts2:17 says, "our sons and daughters shall prophesy."

3. Prophetic dreams is another way God speaks to people. This takes place while we are sleep. This was also talked about in Acts 2:17 when it says your old men shall dream dreams. In Matt. 1:20 God used a dream to assure Joseph, the step father of Jesus, that Mary, his fiancée, was indeed impregnated by a miracle from God. This is something that has never happened before and will never happen again. In Matt. 2:12 God warned the wise men to not return to Herod in a dream in order to tell him the whereabouts of Jesus

when he was a child because Herod wanted to kill him. In Matt. 2:13-19 God warned Joseph to take Jesus and Mary to Egypt to hide from Herod and in the nineteenth verse He let him know in a dream when Herod was dead, so they could return from Egypt. There are also examples in Genesis 37 with Joseph, the son of Jacob and his dreams about ruling as a leader. Also Genesis 41, the dream Pharaoh the leader of Egypt had about the great famine that Joseph interpreted. There are also people like Daniel, in the book of Daniel chapter 2, who interpreted the dream of Nebuchadnezzar the king of Babylon. So not only does God give people dreams but He also has people gifted to interpret those God given dreams and just like prophecy all dreams must be in line with and not violate the word of God. Let me be clear all dreams don't come from God some are our own unconscious thinking and some may be what we ate or watched before we laid down to sleep. All dreams **must** be examined!

4. Prophetic visions are another way God will speak to us. In Acts 2:17 it says, "your young men will see visions." Visions are appearances divinely granted by God. Visions usually take place while a person is awake and conscious. They can be words, pictures, figures, etc. The person who has the vision is conscious of what is happening around them but they still are able to see what God is showing them in the spirit realm. Some examples are Matt. 17:9 when Peter, James, and John saw the transfigured or future body of Jesus after his death, burial, and resurrection in a vision. They also saw a vision of Moses and Elijah talking to Jesus. In Acts 9:10 &12 God shows both Ananias and Paul each other in a vision and instructed Ananias to go lay hands on Paul who was Saul then, a persecutor of the church. At that time Saul (Paul) had an encounter with Jesus on the road to Damascus. Paul was physically blinded at the time he had the vision. In Acts 16:9 Paul also saw a vision of a man in Macedonia saying, "come over here and help us" while he was seeking God for direction of where to evangelize next. God showed John the apostle visions of Jesus and many things to come in the last days before Jesus's return in the Book of Revelations. Also in the Old Testament many prophets such as Isaiah, Jeremiah, Ezekiel, Daniel, Joel, Zechariah, etc., saw visions of things happening as well as things to

come. All visions, just like prophecy, must be tested because all visions don't come from God. Remember Satan is a great deceiver.

5. Prophetic trances are another way God speaks to us. Trances are when our minds', through God's divine intervention, suspends everything around us and although we are awake we only see and hear what divine things the Lord is showing us. It is an ecstasy type state. This is something that rarely happened in the bible but here are some examples. In Numbers 24: 4-16 the soothsayer Balaam fell into a trance while prophesying over Israel the people he was hired to curse but couldn't because God commanded him to bless them. God showed him a vision and Balaam himself said his eyes were open and he was awake but he only saw and heard what God wanted him to hear and see. *In Acts 10:10-13 Peter the apostle was on a roof top praying and hungry, waiting for the food to be prepared when he fell into a trance and saw a vision of a sheet knit together and let down to the four corners of the earth. He saw all manner of four footed beasts of the earth, and wild beasts and creeping things, and fowls of the air when he heard a voice saying arise, kill and eat.* This happened three times. God was showing Peter his inner respect of persons and that Jesus not only came to save the Jews but also the Gentiles. God was sending Peter to a man name Cornelius who was Italian but feared God and needed to hear the gospel of Jesus Christ preached to him; which Peter ended up doing and led Cornelius, and the other Gentiles, to salvation with the instantaneous filling of the Holy Ghost. In Acts 22:17-21 Paul the apostle, fell into a trance while praying in the temple and he saw Jesus who began speaking to him about quickly getting out of Jerusalem because they would not receive him and He (Jesus) was sending him to the Gentiles. Once again all supernatural manifestations must be examined or tested to whether it is of God.

6. Prophetic songs and music are another way God speaks to people. These songs and melodies are not something we previously heard or practiced even though some older songs and melodies do have a prophetic flavor, we are talking about fresh songs and melodies straight from the throne room of Heaven. Psalms 40:3 talks about a new song being put in our mouth. Psalms 33:3 says, "Sing unto him a new song; play skillfully with

a loud noise." In 2 Kings 3:15 Elisha used prophetic music to usher in the presence of God when he asked for a minstrel (player of stringed instruments) then the hand of the Lord came on him to prophesy. In Exodus 15 a prophetic song was sung unto the Lord after God drowned their enemies, the Egyptians, in the Red Sea and after the Israelites passed over unharmed. Ephesians 5:19 talks about spiritual songs, Psalms 32:7 talks about being compassed about with songs of deliverance. Just like anything else songs must be examined because if we are singing unbiblical songs that don't coincide with or violate the scriptures it is not a prophetic song from God. The Holy Spirit will not, I repeat, will not go outside of the word of God.

7. Prophetic dances are also used by God at times to minister to people. I'm not talking about fleshly dances that entice you to sin but dances inspired by God's Spirit. In Exodus 15:20 Miriam, Moses's sister the prophetess, led with a timbrel (tambourine) and the other women joined with timbrels and with dances. In 2 Samuel 6:14-15 David danced before the Lord with all his might when they returned with the ark of the Lord from the house of Obed-Edom with shouting and the sound of the trumpet. Some say David danced out of all his clothes but what he did was take off his kingly garment having on a linen ephod like the Levites and priests. He humbled himself to honor the true King- God. Psalms 149:3 says, "Let them praise him in the dance." Like the other prophetic operations we discussed prophetic dancing must be tested.

8. Prophetic artwork is something new and emerging that God is doing. He is inspiring people in the area of prophetic paintings and other forms of artwork. Aren't we glad God is not limited? He is doing great things in the earth but all these things will honor Father, Jesus and the word of God.

Notes:_____
_____
_____
_____
_____

SECTION III:

PROPHETIC MINISTRIES AND PROPHETIC TEAMS

1. This section is on prophetic ministries and prophetic teams. We will start with prophetic ministries which are ministries called by God to inspire and reveal the ministry of the prophet and its workings and operations. Their goal is to advance the kingdom of God in the earthly realm and raise up prophetic people, prophets, and prophetic teams through God inspired prophetic environments that embrace the glory of God. No they don't just prophesy but they operate in every area of the kingdom of God however, their primary goal is to be God's voice in the earth. Prophetic ministries are emerging today like never before because God is restoring the ministry of the prophet as well as the apostle's ministry back to his church. Those ministries have not been fully embraced by the church today. Some people say we don't need prophets and apostles anymore but men did not give out the gifts to the body Jesus did, and he never took them back; the church has rejected them. Nevertheless, thanks be to God this is the time of restoration and a putting things back in order so God's church can come to the unity of the faith and become that perfect man to the knowledge of the Son of God and unto the measure of the stature of the fullness of Christ (Ephesians 4:13). In other words so the church can become fully what God wants his church to be.

I myself run a prophetic ministry and I see God raising up other pioneers who will not back down and won't give up until the will of God is done and His kingdom comes on earth as it is in heaven. A prophetic ministry is not just designed to affect the church but also our neighborhoods, our communities, our cities, our states, our nations, and to make an impact in the whole earth. We are not just about the four corners of our assembly walls. God has called us out to the market places of our lives. Yes, we are to help make a change in this world we live in. The Kingdom of God will advance and God is raising up prophetic voices to advance it. Prophetic ministries are not about a particular ethnic group of people because the grace of God that brings forth salvation has appeared to all men (Titus 2:11). They are also not about religious positioning or traditions of men that make the word of God of none effect (Mark 7:13). The bible says we can have a form of godliness but deny the power there of from such turn away (2 Timothy 3:5). Prophetic ministries want the power of God to be released but it is God's power that produces change in people. Prophetic ministries are about demonstration and not fancy conversation. Apostle Paul said himself that his preaching was not with enticing words of men's wisdom but with the demonstration of the Spirit and power that their faith should not rest in men but the power of God (1 Cor.2:4-5). Prophetic Ministries will teach and preach God's glory, presence, and his power because that is what we need to bring change to a world full of corruption and perversion. I'm looking forward to what God is doing through his churches in the upcoming days this is going to be an exciting time because those who know their God shall be strong and do exploits (notable deeds) in the earth (Daniel 11:32).

2. Prophetic Ministries will also help to release people into their gifts and callings (1 Tim.4:14).

3. Prophetic Ministries will teach the importance of the Word of God and not elevate a prophetic word over the written word. In other words stress the need to study the bible and to rightly divide the word of truth and not just be eager to receive a prophetic word (2 Tim. 2:15). In Isaiah 8:20 it says, "To the law and testimony: if they speak not according to this word, it is because there is no light in them." In Isaiah 40:8 it says, "the grass withers the flower fades: but the word of God shall stand forever." Jesus said in Matt. 24:35 that his words shall not pass away. I want to make it clear I believe in prophecy and prophesying but most of all I believe God's written word. Any prophecy outside of His word is fallacy and will lead to deception, despair, and false hope because the only true hope we have is in the Word of God. (Also see 2 John 1:9)

4. Prophetic ministries will also stress the glory of God and his power and create an atmosphere conducive for his power and glory. In Exodus 33:18 Moses beseeched God to

shew him God's glory. A prophetic ministry desires to see the glory and presence of God in their midst of the services and in the midst of the lives outside our meeting places. In Psalms 63:1-2 David said that he would, "seek God early and his soul thirsts for God and his flesh longs for him in a dry and thirsty land where no water is and he wanted to see his power and glory , so as he has seen him in the sanctuary." Matthew 5:6 says, "Blessed are they who hunger and thirst after righteousness for they shall be filled." Psalms 145:11 says, "They shall speak of the glory of thy kingdom, and talk of thy power." God is raising up churches that will welcome his glory and power into their midst.

5. Prophetic ministries also will stress the dangers of false preachers, teachers, apostles, prophets, pastors and false spirits to the body of Christ. We must know there is a constant battle between the spirit of truth and the spirit of error. 1 John 4:6 says, "We are of God. He that knoweth God heareth us he that's not of God heareth not us. Hereby know we the spirit of truth and the spirit of error." The apostles of the New Testament understood whomever did not receive the apostles doctrine which came from Jesus himself were not of Christ but had an antichrist spirit operating in them. Matthew 7:15 says, "beware of false prophets which come to you in sheep's clothing but inwardly they are ravening wolves." The bible says we should know them by their fruits. It doesn't matter how gifted they may seem, we must examine the fruit of their character. 2 Peter 2:1-3 says, "there are false prophets and false teachers among us and their heretical teachings and wicked ways and covetous (greedy spirits) with feigned words (formed, wax words) making merchandise (to use a person or a thing for gain) of you. But their judgment is surely coming." I believe some of these false prophets and teachers are using prophecy to do these things or what they call prophesying but I call it *prophelying* because God didn't ordain it. He said in Jeremiah that they prophesied and I never sent them (Jeremiah 23:21). The bible says that they teach things that they ought not for filthy lucre (money) sake (Titus 1:11).

6. Prophetic ministries will teach that prophecy and all operations of the gifts of the Spirit must be judged which we will deal with in the last section of this manual, but now we will go on to discuss Prophetic teams.

7. Prophetic Teams are teams of prophets or prophetic people with the assignment as a cohesive unit to speak forth God's purposes and plans over the lives of his people and at times to the lost souls as the Lord will lead them. In Acts 13:1-2 prophets and teachers ministered to the Lord and fasted. The Holy Ghost spoke and said separate Barnabas and Saul (Paul) for the work they were called to on the evangelistic field. They then fasted and prayed and laid hands on them and sent them away. Here in Acts a team of prophets and teachers fasted and prayed and God spoke and two of them were released for a certain work. Prophetic teams can give godly wisdom through the Spirit of God concerning the work God has called them to. In Acts 11:27 it states that in those days prophets, not one prophet but prophets, went from Jerusalem to Antioch. These were teams of prophets. The Lord showed me this when we developed our prophetic team at the church because he was letting me know the power in unity and agreement. I have seen some awesome powerful things take place when we operate as a prophetic team. In 1 Tim. 4:14 it talks about not neglecting the gift in you which was given to him by prophecy with the laying on of hands of the presbytery or team of elder or team of prophets who spoke over Timothy's life at his ordination for ministry. Notice this is a group of team of people prophesying over Timothy. Now that we have established that God uses prophetic teams we must next examine God's order when it comes to teams being used.

PROPHETIC ORDER FOR PROPHETIC TEAMS

There is a prophetic order when it comes to using prophetic teams. There has always been an order or a right way of doing things when it comes to the house of God. The bible clearly says in 1 Cor.14:40 that all things should be done decently (in a seemly manner) and in order (right order or arrangement). In 1 Cor. 14:29 the scripture says, "Let two or three prophets speak and let the other judge" and we can't override one another while one is speaking but we do have the control to yield to the Spirit of God because the spirit of the prophet is subject to the prophet of that house (1 Cor. 14:30-32); so there is an order. I let our team understand that if we are speaking over an individual or congregation that we only need two or three in a seemly order speaking while the others of us judge. A lot of times we find out God is saying some of the same things to all of the team and then sometimes God will give another team member more to add to the prophetic word but we keep it to two or three as the scripture says. Also we let all team members know If God says nothing to them then say nothing. There is no pressure. This is not a performance. I also wanted to touch on the truth that the spirit of the prophet is subject to the prophet because many people believe they lose control when God uses them. Let me be blunt God will not override your will. We have to make a choice to yield to God when being used by God. He will never make you do anything and anyone who is feeling they are being forced to be used by God they are being controlled by demonic forces because that is unscriptural. This also goes for speaking in tongues. You yield to God if you are on your job and the boss is talking to you about job duties and all you do is speak in tongues you probably will lose your job. I will repeat this it is not God using you. It is a demonic spirit operating and you will need some deliverance. In 1 Cor. 14:33 the bible states that God is not the author of confusion but of peace as in all the churches of the saints. There is a prophetic order we must remember, we can't allow our emotions to overwhelm us and we violate the word of God in the process or we give the devil place to attack us. In 1 Cor.14:26-28 when it comes to speaking in divers tongues in a church setting the same order of two or three applies in an orderly manner and if there be no interpreter we are to keep silent and speak in tongues to ourselves and God because the church is not edified through our tongue speaking. We, the church are edified when those tongues are interpreted as a prophetic word.

Notes:_____

_____

_____

SECTION IV: JUDGING PROPHECY

1. What do we mean when we say to judge prophecy? 1 Thess. 5:21 says to, "prove all things hold fast to that which is good." To prove here means to test, examine, prove, scrutinize, to see whether a thing is genuine or not, to recognize as genuine after examination, to approve, or deem worthy. 1 John 4:1 says, "Beloved believe not every spirit but try the spirit whether they are of God: because many false prophets have gone out into the world." The word try in the scripture means the same as the word prove in 1 Thess. 5:21 and in 1 Cor.14:29 it says, "Two or three prophets should prophesy and let the other judge." That word judge there means to make a distinction, to try, to determine, or to decide. So the word of God is clear we should prove prophecy and every supernatural manifestation that men claim is from God. In 2 Cor. 11:4 says, "If he who cometh preaches another Jesus that we have not preached or if ye receive another spirit which ye have not received or another gospel which ye have not accepted, ye might bear well with them." Apostle Paul here was talking about how the Corinthian church was in danger of losing the simplicity of the gospel and was opening up the door for the false teachers that were coming in to deceive them because they embraced and put up with these false teachers. We must be careful what we accept as truth because anything outside of God's word is just plain wrong!

2. So why are there false amongst the true? People often ask, why are there false apostles, preachers, prophets, teachers, and prophecies among us? My answer is this we have never seen a phony three or four dollar bill because there is no real one. Only something real or original can be copied. God has given the true to his church and the devil will try to imitate and copy that true with something counterfeit, which is something fake with the intent to deceive according to the Webster dictionary. In 1 Cor.11:19 the scripture says, "For there must be heresies among that they which are approved may be made manifest among you." Heresies here are a body of men following their own tenets (doctrines) and

not the doctrines of Christ. The word approved means that which is accepted and pleasing. This word was used to referring to coins and money being genuine.

3. In order to properly judge prophetic utterances we first must determine the source of the word coming to us. There are only three sources from where utterances come.
   a. The source where all true prophetic words come from is God. 2 Peter 1:21 says, "That prophecy in old time came not by the will of man but holy men of God spake as they were moved by the Holy Ghost." So the Holy Spirit moves us or inwardly prompts us to prophesy. The Holy Ghost who is God is the only true source of true prophetic utterances.
   b. The second source where utterances can come from is Satan our adversary, enemy, the devil, and deceiver. In Matthew 16:22-23 Jesus told Peter that Satan was speaking through Peter when Peter rebuked Jesus for telling of his sufferings coming at the hands of the Gentiles before that Jesus had said in Matt. 16:17 that the Father in heaven revealed to Peter that Jesus was the Christ the Son of the living God. So we see from these scriptures a person can be used by God one minute and Satan the next.
   c. The third source where utterances can come from is the human spirit or our own human reasoning. We will find in Jeremiah 14:14, Jeremiah 23:17, 26, Ezek. 13:1-2 examples of prophets prophesying out of their own spirits and own desires of their own hearts.

4. The prophetic word must be bible based meaning it can't violate the principles of God's holy word. Isaiah 8:20 lets us know if they don't speak according to this word then there is no light in them. Here Isaiah was talking about God's people seeking after familiar spirits (mediums) and wizards that peep (whisper and mutter) when they should be seeking God instead of the dead. This includes praying to dead saints for answers. The dead have no portion in this life. We as believers should have no dealings with the occult or any form of witchcraft. This includes horoscopes and psychic hotlines or preachers and teachers who purposefully violate the word intentionally. Deut. 13:1-4 talks about a sign or wonder given by a prophet or dreamer of dreams coming to pass but if that sign or wonder will cause people to go after false gods then it is not of God. Even though it

comes to pass we should not hearken to their words because God is testing our faithfulness to him and his word and if you truly love Him with everything in you.

5. We must examine the word spoken to see if that word glorifies Jesus or men. In John 16:14 the scripture says, "He (Holy Spirit) shall glorify me (Jesus) for he shall receive of mine and show it to you." Any word that does not bring glory to Jesus did not come from God. Apostle Paul said in 1 Cor. 12:3 *that no man speaking by the Spirit of God calleth Jesus accursed and that no man can say Jesus is Lord, but by the Holy Ghost.* Why? Because the Holy Ghost will always exalt Jesus the name that is above every name. Even when God edifies his church Jesus is the head of the church and he always will be honored above all.

6. We must also examine the manner of spirit in which the prophetic word is given. In Luke 9:52-56 the village of Samaritans would not allow Jesus to come through and John and James saw these and asked Jesus, "Should fire be called down from heaven like Elijah did in the book of 1 Kings and burn up that village of people?" Jesus rebuked them saying that they didn't know what manner of spirit they were. He said, he came to save men's lives and not to destroy them. The word *manner* means of what sort of or of what manner of. In other words they had a wrong spirit or attitude about that situation even though they used scripture to justify what they were saying. Some people can prophesy and use the bible but have the wrong motive and spirit. Even when the Lord rebukes people he is still compassionate and loving; not willing that any should perish but come to repentance. Will our Father chasten us? Sure, but always with the heart to restore. He is merciful, truthful, kind, longsuffering and ready to receive. Judgment comes when we reject his invitation to return back to him. Romans 8:1- lets us know that there is no more condemnation to them which are in Christ who walk not after the flesh but after the Spirit. The Holy Spirit is convicting people under this dispensation of grace and truth and not condemning or destroying people.

7. We have to watch to see if the word spoken does come to pass. Once we have met God's conditions of the word given and the season for that word to manifest has also come. Once again prophetic words are conditional and based on the timing of God. If we don't

obey God's instructions and wait on his time that word will not manifest or it will be delayed until we do. Deut. 18:22 says, *"If a prophet speaks in the name of the Lord and it doesn't come to pass or follow, know the Lord hath not spoken but the prophet has spoken presumptuously"* which means out of pride, insolence (being overbearing, cocky) or arrogantly but be not afraid of them. Sometimes the word does not come to pass because the person giving the word may have believed they heard from God but they didn't. It could also mean the person was a false prophet or was speaking falsely for other reasons or motives. Under the Old Testament a false prophet would have lost their life for giving a word that didn't manifest or come to pass (Deut.18:22), but today we are under grace and the prophet's words of today are not infallible in the New Testament. Prophecy in the New Testament must be judged because it is not perfect as a matter of truth the bible says in 1 Cor. 13:9 says, "for we know in part and prophecy also in part," no one knows everything and men can be wrong. God himself is perfect, His gifts are perfect but the recipients of the gifts are being perfected. Therefore we are subject to misinterpret something as being from God and it is not from him.

8. What is the character of the person giving the word? Remember Matt. 7:15-21 talks about wolves in sheep's clothing and goes on further to say we shall know them by the fruit they bear because good trees don't bear corrupt fruit and corrupt trees don't bear good fruit. We must learn to examine the character of people because the character tells us a lot about the person. However, sometimes we get caught up in a person's charisma and excited about their performance, forgetting to ask, what kind of life do they live? Do they have holy integrity outside the church pulpit? Does their teaching and preaching stay in line with the bible? According to 1 John 4:2-3 do they confess that Jesus has come in the flesh if not that is the spirit of antichrist operating in them? Do they have a full understanding of who Jesus is? As when he asked his disciples, "Who do men say I am and they answered some say Elias, Jeremiah, John the Baptist, etc. Then he asked them, who do you say I am? And Peter said that thou art the Christ the son of the living God." Jesus is God. He was born of a virgin. He died on the cross after being beaten, pierced in his side and endured other horrific acts. He was buried and raised from the dead after the

third day and now sits on the right hand of God the Father in Heaven. He also will return to the earth again the second time. This is the Jesus of the bible and a person sent by God will be convinced of these biblical truths. We must examine a person's character by the fruit they bear.

9. Does the word given bring confirmation to what God has already been saying to us? Romans 8:16 says, "The Spirit bears witness to our spirits we are the children of God." In other words the Holy Spirit will bear witness to our spirits that he is speaking to us. 1 John 2:20 says we do have an unction (anointing) from the holy one to know all things. We have an anointing on the inside of us as believers to know when something is God if we would listen to the still small voice of the Holy Spirit speaking to our spirit man or what some may call an inner witness. 2 Cor. 13:1 says, "Out of the mouth of two or three witnesses shall every word be established." God will confirm his spoken word through others. However, we must remember people can see things God shows them, hear things God tells them and still let their emotions get in the way. An example of this is in Acts 21:4 some disciples said to Paul, through the Spirit, that he should not go up to Jerusalem. What they saw or heard in the spirit was right but their emotions got on the way of the interpretation. Paul had also gotten the same word of his future suffering from Agabus the prophet in Acts 21:10-14 as well as many others (Acts 20:22-24) but Paul still had to hear God for himself and he knew the Holy Spirit was leading him to Jerusalem. I said all that to say this, we must know what God is speaking to our hearts and be led by the Spirit of God (Romans 8:14).

Notes:_____
_____
_____
_____
_____
_____

THE CONCLUSION

I believe that we are truly in a prophetic time where God is raising up apostolic and prophetic leaders to impart to the body of Christ a true apostolic and prophetic spirit that will bring transformation and reformation (restore things to proper order) to the true church of our Lord and Savior Jesus Christ. My prayer is that our God will unleash his glory and power like never before upon his people and that we may carry it to the uttermost parts of the earth.

To all who read this manual, I pray you grow in leaps and bounds in your prophetic gifting, grace and calling. May prophetic wisdom, insight, knowledge and understanding abundantly increase beyond what you can think or imagine as you go from faith to faith and glory to glory through and by the Holy Spirit. God bless you all, be encouraged and I love you with the love of Christ. As Apostle Paul would say grace unto you, and peace from God the Father and the Lord Jesus Christ.

PLEASE USE THE REST OF THIS MANUAL TO WRITE WHAT YOU'VE LEARNED AND WHAT THE HOLY SPIRIT IS SAYING TO YOU.

WWW.PropheticKingdomMinistries.com

ABOUT THE AUTHOR

April 30th 1995 the day we gave our lives to the Lord Jesus at Trinity Holiness Church. As with any growth experience there is a thirst for knowledge, with that we visited other ministries. A friend recommended that we visit PMOD where Apostle Hopkins is founder and overseer.

July 1, 1995 Apostle Thomas Sturgis presided over my wife and I in the GOD ordained union called marriage. During that same time we began attending Pilgrim Ministry of Deliverance where we became members. Through our union we have three children and one granddaughter.

Through faithful service I was soon asked to be the armor bearer for Apostle Hopkins and Bishop Bailey. I humbly accepted, and this lead to more opportunities for GOD to use me. Soon I began to teaching the Adult Sunday School class. I taught Sunday school for nine years during this time I began my studies as a minister a year later my beloved wife began her studies as a minister.

As I studied, taught and served faithfully the Lord began to deal with my heart about Prophetic calling and the duties of a Pastor. The Lord's word was confirmed through his servants and church leaders. In 2006 my spiritual fathers' Apostle Hopkins and Bishop Levin Bailey told me to start looking for a building. We found a building in September 2006 in Dover Delaware. On October 22, 2006 I was ordained at Pilgrim's Ministry of Deliverance as Pastor of Prophetic Kingdom Ministries. The Ministry officially started November 5, 2006.

On August 8, 2008 through the leading of the Holy Spirit we moved to the Milford, DE area in a 2500 square foot building which we are now in this present day.

www.ingramcontent.com/pod-product-compliance
Lightning Source LLC
Chambersburg PA
CBHW080445110426
42743CB00016B/3287